W9-AVK-139

MARS
WA

CONTEMPORARY LIVES

BRUNO MARS

POP SUPERSTAR

ABDO
Publishing Company

BRUNO MARS

by Stephanie Watson

CREDITS

Published by ABDO Publishing Company, PO Box 398166, Minneapolis, MN 55439. Copyright © 2014 by Abdo Consulting Group, Inc. International copyrights reserved in all countries. No part of this book may be reproduced in any form without written permission from the publisher. The Essential Library™ is a trademark and logo of ABDO Publishing Company.

Printed in the United States of America,
North Mankato, Minnesota
082013
012014

 THIS BOOK CONTAINS AT LEAST 10% RECYCLED MATERIALS.

Editor: Megan Anderson
Series Designer: Emily Love

Photo credits: Shutterstock Images, cover, 3, 32, 46, 69; AP Images, 6, 18, 59, 67, 97 (bottom); Matt Sayles/AP Images, 9, 50, 62, 76, 98; Brian Zak/Sipa Press/AP Images, 11; Columbia Pictures/Photofest, 14; Seth Poppel/Yearbook Library, 24, 27; Amy Sussman/Invision/AP, 38; Jeff Christensen/AP Images, 41; Chris Pizzello/AP Images, 42, 97 (top); Richard Drew/AP Images, 52, 96; Jeff Kravitz/Film Magic//Getty Images, 54; Getty Images, 72, 98 (bottom); Ian West/Press Association/AP Images, 78; Ilya S. Savenok/Getty Images, 85; Rex Features/AP Images, 86, 94, 100; John Shearer/Invision/AP Images, 90, 99 (bottom)

Library of Congress Control Number: 2013946053

Cataloging-in-Publication Data

Watson, Stephanie.
 Bruno Mars: pop superstar / Stephanie Watson.
   p. cm. -- (Contemporary lives)
Includes bibliographical references and index.
ISBN 978-1-62403-225-7
1. Mars, Bruno, 1985- --Juvenile literature. 2. Musicians--United States--Biography--Juvenile literature. 1. Title.
782.42164092--dc23
[B]

2013946053

CONTENTS

Mars worked his way up in the music industry as a songwriter and producer before finding success as a solo artist.

CHAPTER 1

New York City Is on Mars

||||||||||||||||||||||||||||||||||||||||||||||||||||||||||||||||

Everyone who was anyone in the music business was at New York City's Madison Square Garden on December 10, 2010. They were there to perform at the Jingle Ball, a celebrity-filled bash held by New York radio station Z100 each year to celebrate the start of the holiday season.

At one point in the show, a big red box wrapped in a gold bow was pushed out onto the stage. Singer Katy Perry popped out wearing a nutcracker costume. She launched into a high-energy performance of her hit, "Hot N Cold." In another memorable moment, teen heartthrob Justin Bieber lovingly sang "Baby" to the girls in the crowd, every line sending the audience into a near-riot of screams. Other pop stars such as Enrique Iglesias, Selena Gomez, and Taio Cruz also took their turns playing to the packed crowd.

Someone new was also set to take the stage that night: Bruno Mars, a singer-songwriter from Honolulu, Hawaii. The new sensation had recently burst onto the music scene singing hooks on hit songs by hip-hop artists B.o.B. and Travie McCoy. Mars just released his first solo album, *Doo-Wops & Hooligans*, on October 5, 2010, after spending five years struggling to make it in the music business.

STRUCK BY FAME

Even after working hard for several years to make it in the music industry, Mars was still in awe of his newfound fame. "It's a rare thing that happens, especially in this day, where it's real hard to sell albums," he told *Billboard* magazine. "I'm traveling to places that I've never even heard of and there are all these people singing the songs back—and English is not even their first language."[1]

Mars has had successful collaborations with artists such as B.o.B., *left*.

CROWD PLEASER

The stage went dark. The crowd murmured in anticipation. The emcee announced: "Ladies and gentlemen, please welcome to the stage . . . Bruno Mars!"[2] The theme from the 1968 science fiction movie *2001: A Space Odyssey* began to play. "Da . . . da . . . da . . . da-DA!"[3] Mars walked confidently onto the stage, wearing a jean jacket, black pants, and gray fedora. He stepped up to the microphone and stretched his arms up to the sky in victory. The crowd cheered in response.

Mars and his band performed "Grenade" and "Just the Way You Are," two songs from his debut album. Most of the approximately 18,000 fans in the audience already knew all the lyrics and were singing every word right along with him. Mars flashed a smile—it was obvious he was enjoying every minute of his breakthrough performance.

Though he was just 25 years old, Mars could command the stage as well as any veteran performer. Despite his youth, Mars had been playing in front of an audience for more than two decades. He'd started in the music business at age four, performing Elvis impersonations with his father's doo-wop band in Hawaiian hotels.

BRIGHT YOUNG STAR

As the crowd at Madison Square Garden watched Mars perform, it was obvious he was so much more than just a singer. John Janick, former copresident of Mars's record label Elektra Records, has called him a "quadruple threat."[4] "He's a writer,

Mars often wears a fedora during his performances.

a producer, an amazing singer and an amazing performer—on top of that he just has a great personality," Janick said.[5]

Even as such a young artist, Mars has a rare magnetism attractive to both fans and other celebrities. Backstage at the Jingle Ball, Justin Bieber told Mars how much he wanted to work with him. Later, Mars joked around with rapper Flo Rida: "Who you dating now, Flo? You've got a different supermodel every time I see you!"[6]

As Mars left Madison Square Garden that night, he confidently strode through the hallway announcing, "I want a hug from every girl here!"[7] The girls lining the hallway were more than willing. Outside, another crowd of girls screamed as Mars appeared. Playing with the crowd, Mars ducked behind his van. The girls quieted down. Then he popped his head above the hood of the van. The girls started screaming again. He ducked his head behind the van. They stopped screaming. It was like flipping a light switch. "Ha, ha! How cool is that?" he asked the reporter who was with him.[8]

> **"Writing with Bruno, it's like having a conversation with one of your friends. You've got to be direct. You don't have to figure out how to say something, you just say it."**[9]
>
> *—B.O.B.*

Mars knew this was his moment. He had come to Los Angeles just after his high school graduation to pursue his music career. At the time, he had very little money—but he had a huge dream. He spent more than five years performing in local bars, writing songs for other artists, and once even selling his guitars for rent money. Now he had made his dream a reality. He had a string of hit songs and a legion of fans around the world. Mars's success was about to be out of this world.

||||||||||

Dressed as a little Elvis, Bruno had a brief cameo in the 1992 film *Honeymoon in Vegas*.

CHAPTER 2

The Littlest Elvis

IIIIIIIIIIIIIIIIIIIIIIIIIIII

O n October 8, 1985, Peter Gene Hernandez Jr. was born in Honolulu, Hawaii. When Peter arrived, music was already in his blood. His father, Peter "Dr. Doo-Wop" Hernandez, was a Jewish–Puerto Rican drummer-bandleader from Brooklyn, New York. His mother, Bernadette, was a singer-dancer who had moved to Hawaii from the Philippines in 1968, when she was ten. In 1977,

Doo-wop is a style of music that emerged from the inner cities in the 1950s. Groups of teenagers harmonized on street corners and in churches. They blended sounds from rhythm and blues (R&B) and jazz music. Because many of these singers were too poor to afford instruments, doo-wop groups sang a cappella. They created the rhythms and harmonies with their voices instead of with drums, horns, and guitars.

Hernandez moved to Hawaii, where he met Bernadette at a Polynesian revue.

Hernandez was a Latin percussionist and Bernadette was a hula dancer. They eventually got married. Music was so much a part of the family's life Hernandez dimmed the lights in the delivery room and played a cassette of oldies music while his wife was in labor with Peter Jr.

Peter Jr. soon got the unusual nickname of Bruno because he reminded his father of professional wrestler Bruno Sammartino. "Bruno was always so confident, independent, really strong-willed and kind of a brute—hence the name Bruno, and it kind of just stuck," said Bruno's older sister, Jaime.[1]

A MUSICAL FAMILY

Bruno was the third of six children. He has four sisters: Jaime, Tiara, Tahiti, and Presley (named after famous rock-and-roll singer Elvis). He also has one brother, Eric. Jaime and Eric are older than Bruno, while Tiara, Tahiti, and Presley are younger. Bruno grew up surrounded by music, and all of his siblings sing and play instruments. "At every family gathering all of us would be singing, and he would be the biggest ham," recalled Bruno's uncle, John Valentine.[2]

In the early 1980s, Bruno's father had his own doo-wop vocal group called the Love Notes, which performed at clubs around Waikiki, a tourist-friendly town on Honolulu's southern shore. The act was so successful, Peter bought his family a big house in Kahala, a wealthy suburb of Honolulu. Bruno had a huge room of his own, which he quickly filled with all kinds of musical instruments.

The Love Notes show started as an a cappella musical act. But by the mid-1980s, it had expanded into a full-scale Las Vegas–style musical revue, complete with celebrity impersonations,

Bruno studied Elvis's signature movements and incorporated them into his impersonation.

music, and dancing. By age two, little Bruno was already singing in tune and clamoring to get on stage. "All my kids sing but they're shy," said Bernadette, who also performed in the show. "You put them on stage and they choke, but Bruno wanted to be on stage."[3]

A HIT IMPERSONATION

Even though he was still in diapers, Bruno's star potential was clear. By far, Bruno's favorite part of the show was his uncle's Elvis Presley

ELVIS PRESLEY

Singer and actor Elvis Presley was born on January 8, 1935, in Tupelo, Mississippi. He is the best-selling solo artist in the history of popular music. Elvis is considered a pioneer of rock and roll, which combines sounds from R&B, country, and gospel music. Often called "The King of Rock and Roll," he gave high-energy performances, rotating his hips to the rhythm of the music. His first single, "That's All Right" was released in 1954. His first Number 1 album, *Elvis Presley*, was released in 1956 and includes the Number 1 hit "Heartbreak Hotel."

Elvis acted in movies such as *Love Me Tender* (1956), *Jailhouse Rock* (1957), *Blue Hawaii* (1961), and *Viva Las Vegas* (1964). But his musical relevance began to decline, so in 1969, Elvis launched a musical comeback, including a monthlong string in Las Vegas, Nevada. Signatures of these performances were his long sideburns and beaded jumpsuits, which spawned countless impersonations. But his addiction to prescription drugs led to his death from heart failure on August 16, 1977.

Bruno's father was such an Elvis Presley fan, he opened an entire store devoted to the King of Rock and Roll. The shop was located in Waikiki and sold Elvis T-shirts, photos, movie posters, old concert tickets, and other memorabilia.

impersonation, which left the girls in the audience screaming for him. "And as a young kid, you're like, 'I want that,'" Bruno said.[4]

Bruno watched his uncle perform on stage, and also studied videos of Elvis to learn the legendary singer's moves. He would lock himself in his room, rehearsing the moves again and again. He wanted to get in on the family act.

> **"Being Little Elvis was incredible for me. Following him taught me so much about showmanship and swagger. He'd get up on stage and just rock the place. I try to capture that feel when I perform."[6]**
>
> —BRUNO MARS

"I'd always ask my dad, 'Yo, bring me up onstage,'" Bruno said.[5] Finally, when he was four, he got his chance. During the Love Notes performance at a Sheraton hotel opening in Japan, Peter brought his son up onstage. Bruno shook his legs and sang just like Elvis. The crowd went wild. Back at the Sheraton in Waikiki, Bruno did his Elvis impression again in the hotel's Esprit Lounge. He wore a spangled Elvis costume his mother had made him for Halloween. She teased his curly hair up into a tiny pompadour. He sang and grinded his hips to renditions of Elvis's "Hound Dog," "Blue Suede Shoes," and "All Shook Up." "Didn't sound, didn't look anything like Elvis, but . . . it was a big gimmick, and tourists ate it up," he said, laughing.[7]

Bruno quickly gained a reputation as the world's youngest Elvis impersonator. Television news network CNN did a segment on him. In 1990, Bruno was featured in a British documentary about Elvis impersonators called *Viva Elvis*. When the producers asked what he liked about Elvis, Bruno responded, "I like his singing and his dance

MUSICAL INFLUENCES ||||||||||||||||||||||||||||||||||||||||||||||||||||||||||||||||

Bruno was not just a novelty act. He was a real musician from a very young age. He got his musical inspiration from his favorite performers, including Stevie Wonder, Michael Jackson, Sting, and Freddie Mercury. Many of his other idols, such as Chuck Berry, Little Richard, and James Brown, were stars long before he Wilson and James Brown—they were like, 'Watch me dance; I'm going to set this whole place on fire,'" Bruno said. "You see that as a kid, you're just blown away."[8] Bruno learned how to dance from his idols. He taught himself how to play the drums, piano, and guitar. And he learned how to strum a bass and ukulele.

and his lips," curling his own upper lip into a copy of Elvis's famous sneer.[9] "I loved it. Ate it up," Bruno later said of the attention.[10]

In 1992, at age six, Bruno landed a cameo role as Little Elvis in the movie *Honeymoon in Vegas*, starring actors Sarah Jessica Parker and Nicolas Cage. Even though he was only on screen for about 20 seconds, his hip-swinging version of "Can't Help Falling in Love" was a scene stealer.

MUSICIAN IN THE MAKING

Regardless of his age, Bruno was a total professional. In elementary school, he played two shows a night with his family's band. Music consumed Bruno's life. While attending Robert Louis Stevenson Middle School in Honolulu, all he could think about was his next performance and, eventually, becoming a successful recording artist.

When Bruno was around age 11, his musical family hit a sour note when his parents divorced. Bruno's sisters went to live with their mother, while he stayed with his father. The family band also broke up. For the first time, money became tight. Bruno and his father moved to Manoa, a less affluent suburb of Honolulu, which Bruno called "the slums of Hawaii."[11] At one point they were almost totally broke. But with the last money Peter had, he bought his son a $115 Fender guitar.

||||||||||

ELVIS COSTUMES

Elvis Presley was known for the over-the-top costumes he wore on stage. In the late 1960s and early 1970s, he was often seen wearing a rhinestone- or metal-studded jumpsuit. Each of the jumpsuits had a high collar, bell-bottoms, an oversized matching belt, and a cape. Elvis's costumes were the creations of famed designer Bill Belew. Over his almost 50-year career, Belew also designed looks for artists such as Gloria Estefan, the Osmonds, and the Jacksons.

In order to capture Elvis, Bruno had to get his own look right without a famous designer to make his outfits for him. Also, it wasn't easy to find an Elvis costume small enough to fit a four-year-old's body. So Bruno's mother Bernadette made his stage outfits for him. "She was a killer seamstress," Bruno said.[12] The costumes—including the black leather suit from Elvis's 1968 comeback special and the white jumpsuit with the huge eagle emblazoned across the front from his 1973 Hawaii concert—were all authentic replicas.

Bruno discovered his impersonations and musical talents impressed girls in high school.

CHAPTER 3

Launching a Music Career

||||||||||||||||||||||||||||||||||||||||||||||||||||||||||||||||||||||||||||||||||||

Performing at a very early age made Bruno even more comfortable on stage than he was in school. By the time he was a teenager, he was doing perfect impersonations of popular R&B singers Ray Charles, Frankie Lymon, and Jackie Wilson at his father's reopened musical revue. His father taught him how to play classic rock songs by Chuck Berry, Carlos Santana, and the Ventures on the guitar. Bruno also mastered singer Michael Jackson's dance moves and sound.

Classic R&B was not the only genre of music that inspired Bruno. He also followed modern hip-hop acts such as Dr. Dre, the Neptunes, and Timbaland, as well as rock-and-roll legends such as Jimi Hendrix. At age 16, he taught himself how to play Hendrix's wailing guitar version of "The Star-Spangled Banner," which had blown away crowds at the 1969 Woodstock music festival in upstate New York. By his teenage years, Bruno had found another important reason to learn how to play music like his idols. "I'd see things and say, 'Man, if I could do that, I'm sure I could impress a lot of girls,'" he said.[1]

"Ever since I was a kid this was all I wanted to do. I've wanted to do music. I wanted to sing. It's all I know."[2]

—BRUNO MARS

Bruno's hair was one way he stood out in high school.

STUDENT BY DAY, STAR BY NIGHT

During the day, Bruno attended Roosevelt High School in Honolulu. At night, he pursued his music. He performed with his father's act and also formed a band called the School Boys with classmates Joey Kaalekahi, Dwayne Andres, and Reid Kobashigawa. The School Boys sang classic oldies such as "I'm So Young" and "Why Do Fools Fall in Love?" at the Ilikai Hotel in Honolulu.

When Mars was in high school, he had quite a large hairdo, which is evident in school photos. In his 2003 Roosevelt High School senior class photo, Mars appears in a tux with a full head of curls. As his fame grew, Mars changed to a pompadour hairstyle, where his hair was combed into a mound in the front. But eventually he switched back to a shorter head of curls, because the pompadour took too long to maintain. "It was becoming too much," Mars said. "Now I wake up, shower, and leave my hair as is."[5]

Bruno and the School Boys would perform the 8:00 p.m. show, then head home to bed to rest up for school the next day.

Bruno's music also started to extend into his school life. At a pep rally during his sophomore year of high school, Bruno performed Ginuwine's song "Pony." His performance had the girls screaming. "After that, I walked around the halls like I was Sinatra," Bruno said.[3]

While he was still in high school, Bruno got a job as the opening act for a musical magic show called "The Magic of Polynesia" at the Holiday Inn Waikiki Beachcomber Hotel. Bruno described it as "David Copperfield meets hula."[4] Bruno made $75 a night—a lot of money for someone still in high school. He performed approximately ten songs to warm up the crowd for the main act—a dinner show combining the magic of legendary illusionist John Hirokawa with traditional Polynesian songs and dances. "I was background music while people were eating dinner," Bruno later told *Rolling Stone*.[6] He also had another gig at a celebrity revue performing a near-perfect impersonation of Michael Jackson.

BRUNO IS FROM MARS

Eventually, Bruno Hernandez reinvented himself by adopting a new last name. He joked with a reporter about his reasons for choosing his stellar name, saying, "The Mars came up just because I felt like I didn't have no pizzazz, and a lot of girls say I'm out of this world, so I was like I guess I'm from Mars."[7]

But his real reason for ditching the name Hernandez was he didn't want to be seen solely as a Hispanic music act singing Spanish-language songs. He imagined record company executives saying to him, "Your last name's Hernandez, maybe you should do this Latin music, this Spanish music . . . Enrique [Iglesias]'s so hot right now."[8] To make sure he could perform the type of music he wanted to sing, Bruno Hernandez became Bruno Mars.

MOVING UP—AND OUT

In the spring of 2003, Mars graduated from high school. He was 17 years old. Both his older siblings, Eric and Jaime, had already moved from Hawaii to Los Angeles, California. Bruno decided to follow them and pursue his music career in the center of the entertainment industry.

He moved in with his sister, hoping for his big break. However, becoming a famous musician was not as easy as he had envisioned. "You think it's like the movies, like you get signed and [famous rappers] Pharrell and Timbaland are working with you. But it wasn't like that," he said.[9] Bruno realized his talent would only get him so far. To go the rest of the way to fame, he'd have to work hard and even write songs. Mars later said,

> I only started writing songs when I moved up to L.A., because when I was in Hawaii I never really needed to . . . It's not like what you see in movies, where you walk into a record company and you're given all these great songs to sing. You have to write the song the world is going to want to hear and play over and over again.[10]

> "Coming from Hawaii, [Los Angeles] was a whole 'nother thing. It's so much faster than where I'm from. We don't got billboards in Hawaii."[12]
>
> —*BRUNO MARS*

Mars wrote a bunch of songs and then made a demo recording. His sister managed to get the demo in front of Mike Lynn, an executive at Aftermath Entertainment. The record label is owned by successful rapper-producer Dr. Dre. "My demo was terrible, I sounded like a chipmunk," Mars said.[11] Yet Lynn heard something he liked. In 2004, he signed 18-year-old Mars to a $100,000 deal with Universal Motown Records, part of the Universal Music Group label.

|||||||||||

After being dropped suddenly from his record label, Mars started performing in bars in the San Fernando Valley.

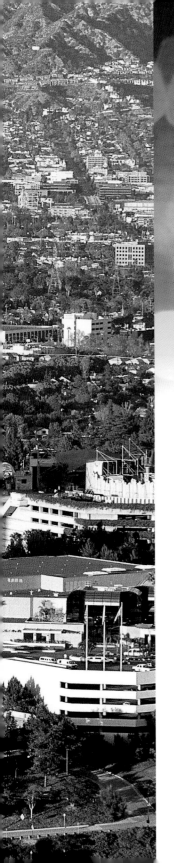

CHAPTER 4

Struggling in Los Angeles

||||||||||||||||||||||||||||||||||||||||||||||||||||||||||||

At just 18 years old, Mars had signed with one of the biggest record companies in the industry: Universal Motown Records. He was on the same music label as R&B legends Marvin Gaye, Smokey Robinson, Diana Ross, and his musical hero, Michael Jackson. But his good fortune would not be long-lived.

||||||||||||||||||||||||||||||||||

MOTOWN RECORDS

In 1959, a time when African Americans still struggled for equality in the United States, an aspiring young songwriter and producer named Berry Gordy Jr. launched a new record label in Detroit, Michigan. He called it Motown Records, a contraction of *town* and *motor*, inspired by Detroit's famous nickname, "the Motor City."

Gordy signed young local artists such as Smokey Robinson, Martha and the Vandellas, Marvin Gaye, and Mary Wells. He created the signature Motown sound—a blend of jazz, pop, and African-American church music. In 1960, the label had its first Number 1 R&B hit with the song "Shop Around" by Smokey Robinson and the Miracles. By the mid-1960s, Gordy's label had a string of hits.

Over the next couple of decades, Motown added more big names—including the Commodores, Stevie Wonder, and Rick James. In 1988, Gordy sold his label to MCA and Boston Partners. Today, Motown is still cranking out hit records, but it's part of the much larger Universal Music Group.

DROPPED

Mars recorded one demo with Mike Lynn. After a year, Universal Motown dropped him without releasing a single CD. The company was worried it would not be able to market a young artist who did not fit into any one musical genre. "No

rapper Kanye West—which forced Sex Panther to break up.

BROKE

Mars was 19 years old. He was 2,500 miles (4,023 km) away from his hometown and totally broke. His record company had dropped him, his band had dissolved, and he was so poor he could not even afford to fill the gas tank of his Jeep Cherokee. To earn enough cash to pay the bills, Mars sold his guitars at local pawnshops.

By this time, Mars had moved to his own apartment on Mansfield Avenue in a rough section of Los Angeles. "It was really bad," he said.[9] One day, he was about to pull into his parking space when he saw a homeless man using it as a toilet. "It was just foul," Mars said.[10]

Money became so scarce Mars considered moving back to Hawaii. He knew going back to his family would provide him with comfort, support, and financial security. Ultimately, Mars decided to stick it out in Los Angeles. "If I had moved back to Hawaii, I felt I never would have made it

These days, Bruno Mars is hardly ever seen without a fedora. The fedora is a type of hat first made popular in the 1960s. Where did Mars's fedora come from? During those difficult months when he and his band were performing in bars, he used to gamble on card games to earn extra cash. One very successful night, Mars won $600. With his earnings, he decided to go into the casino shop. He saw a gray fedora on display. Mars bought it, and he still wears one like it today.

back up here. I would have been at the Polynesian Review with a ukulele and an Aloha shirt, probably singing Elvis tunes," he said.[11] "I just felt like I couldn't come back yet."[12] This risky choice would make the difference between Mars playing in local clubs for the rest of his life and becoming an international superstar.

||||||||||

A broke Mars searched for ways to stay relevant in the music industry.

Mars formed the Smeezingtons
with Philip Lawrence, *left*,
and Ari Levine, *center*.

CHAPTER 5

From Singer to Songwriter

||||||||||||||||||||||||||||||||||||||||||||||||||||||||||||||||||||||||||||

I n 2005, Bruno Mars was broke and struggling in Los Angeles. But his songwriting had improved, and he was slowly learning about the music business. Combining artistic forces with another aspiring musician would be just what Mars needed to turn his sagging career around.

That musician was songwriter-producer Philip Lawrence, whom

The meeting between Bruno Mars and Philip Lawrence resulting in hit songwriting trio the Smeezingtons almost didn't happen. Lawrence was so poor he could barely afford the two-dollar bus fare to meet Mars for their first recording session. "I had to get two buses and it cost me the last money I had. It turned out to be the best two dollars I've ever spent," Lawrence said.[2]

Mars met while he was still signed to Universal Motown. "We immediately hit it off because we have such a similar musical sensibility—we're very melody-driven," Lawrence said.[1] The two men teamed up. Mars played the instruments and wrote lyrics, while Lawrence came up with the melodies. Producer-songwriter Ari Levine joined them to form a songwriting-producing powerhouse trio.

||||||||||||||||||||||||||||||||||||||||||||||||||

THE SMEEZINGTONS

The songwriting-production trio of Mars, Lawrence, and Levine called themselves the Smeezingtons. "Smeez" is a play on the word *smash*, the kind of hit the group hoped to have. "We used to always say in the studio, 'Yo, this is going to be a smash!' Mars explained to *Entertainment Weekly*. "And then it turned into, 'This is a smeeze!' Then, 'This is a Smeezington.'"[3]

As producers, the Smeezingtons acted as creative directors of a song. They selected the musicians, the arrangements, and coordinated the recording sessions. As songwriters, they collaborated to find the right melody and lyrics. At first, their goal was to produce a hit for Mars. "Bruno always had the voice," Lawrence said. "But we just needed to put together the right song and the right package for him."[4] The songs they wrote had catchy lyrics and big choruses bound to get attention. And the songs did get attention—but not for Mars.

Brandon Creed, vice president of artists and repertoire (A&R) for Epic Records, asked to buy

"I had to put in my time. . . . As a producer and writer I'd write a song and say 'dang, I wish I could keep that one for me,' but you have bills to pay, so you do what you have to do. You just wait for the day when somebody will say 'Bruno, you're ready.'"[5]

—*BRUNO MARS*

Flo Rida's "Right Round" was the Smeezingtons's first hit.

one of the Smeezingtons's songs, "Lost." He wanted Menudo, a Puerto Rican boy band, to record the song. "I was like, 'No way, just sign me,'" Bruno said. "They said, 'We'll give you 20 grand,' and I said, 'Here's your song, what else do you need?'"[6]

Despite the money, Mars was disappointed. He wanted to be the main act—not a behind-the-scenes songwriter. But he soon realized writing hit songs for other artists was a way for him to sneak into the music business.

A STRING OF HITS

Twenty-year-old Mars and the Smeezingtons were determined to write a hit song. "We knew that we could do it. If we kept going, if we kept trying, if we kept pushing, we are going to write the song that's going to change our lives," he said. "Yeah. [We] wrote a few songs that changed our lives."[7]

The song that put the Smeezingtons on the map was "Right Round," which they wrote for rapper Flo Rida. The trio sampled the melody from the 1980s hit song by Dead or Alive, "You Spin Me Round (Like a Record)." Mars and Lawrence wrote the lyrics in approximately two minutes. Mars's friend Ke$ha sang the chorus. Although critics hated "Right Round," the public loved it when

KE$HA

During the lean months after Mars's record company dropped him, he stayed in contact with another singer-songwriter, Ke$ha. Mars and Ke$ha bonded while they were struggling to make it in the music industry. "Ke$ha and I were signed to the same management; we'd call each other up and see what the other was working on, which was usually nothing," Mars said.[8] Ke$ha eventually released her own solo album, *Animal*, in January 2010. It debuted at Number 1 on *Billboard* and features Number 1 single "Tik Tok."

it was released in early 2009. It was Mars's first Number 1 song as a songwriter. "That was our first taste of what could really happen with a hit . . . ," Mars said.[9]

The Smeezingtons wrote the song "Wavin' Flag" for Somali-Canadian hip-hop artist K'naan. The song appeared on K'naan's 2009 album, *Troubadour*. "Wavin' Flag" became a worldwide hit, and it was Coca-Cola's anthem for the 2010 FIFA World Cup soccer series. The song "One Day,"

"[FORGET] YOU"

By the time he wrote "[Forget] You" with Cee Lo Green, Mars was already an established songwriter. And Green was no newcomer, either. He'd first risen to fame in the early 1990s with the southern rap act, Goodie Mob. Like Mars, Green struggled on the road to success. Then in 2006, he became half of the musical duo Gnarls Barkley with producer Danger Mouse. Green hit Number 2 on the *Billboard* Hot 100 music chart with the Gnarls Barkley song "Crazy."

When Mars and Green went into the studio together, the songwriting process flowed easily. Mars came up with the melody, which he gave a 1960s R&B sound. Then he and Green wrote the lyrics collaboratively. "One of us would say half of a line, the other would finish it, just going like that till the song was done," Mars said.[10] Then, he said, "When Cee Lo got in there and sang, we all got the chills."[11] "[Forget] You" peaked at Number 2 on the *Billboard* Hot 100

which Mars and the Smeezingtons wrote for reggae singer Matisyahu, also became a sort of anthem. Television network NBC played the song during its coverage of the 2010 Winter Olympics.

Mars also wrote "Young, Wild & Free" for rappers Snoop Dogg and Wiz Khalifa. But his collaboration with singer Cee Lo Green resulted in the successful, and controversial, 2010 song, "[Forget] You." The song went viral, thanks to a popular music video and a performance by actress Gwyneth Paltrow on the popular television show *Glee*. "[Forget] You" was such a major hit many people wondered why Mars did not record it himself.

||||||||||||||||||||||||||||||||||||||||||||||||||||||||||||

MARS FINALLY GETS HEARD

After taking a backseat to other recording artists for a few years, Mars decided to put his own voice on a record. He sang the chorus on the song "Nothin' On You," which he cowrote with rapper B.o.B. The song was released on B.o.B.'s 2010 debut album, *B.o.B. Presents: The Adventures of Bobby Ray*.

Mars performs at the 2010 Teen Choice Awards.

The first time Mars heard his own voice on the radio was while he was driving around Inglewood, California. "Nothin' On You" came on the local radio station. The song eventually went to Number 1 on the *Billboard* Hot 100 chart. "Nothin' On You" was nominated for three Grammy Awards in 2011, including Record of the Year.

Mars also lent his voice to another song he'd written, "Billionaire," which was recorded by singer-rapper Travie McCoy. The acoustic reggae song was inspired by Mars's frustration at his lack of career success. "I was tired of spending half my day worrying about what I can and can't spend on whatever," he told *Forbes*.[12] So he dreamed about what his life would be like if he were a superstar, saying,

> I wouldn't have to worry about, you know, 'I can't afford to get breakfast, so I'll wait until lunchtime to eat.' If I was a billionaire, none of that would matter. I'd be eating diamond cereal.[13]

With "Billionaire," Mars was on his way to the superstardom he daydreamed about. The song sold 2 million singles in just two months. And it would finally help launch Mars's solo career.

|||||||||

"NOTHIN' ON YOU"

Mars made his record debut singing the chorus of "Nothin' On You." The song was inspired by his sisters' dating experiences. "I have four sisters, and all my life I've heard about what their boyfriends do and don't do," Mars said.[14] Mars wrote this chorus for the song: "Beautiful girls, all over the world/I could be chasin' but my time would be wasted/They got nothin' on you, baby."[15]

"Nothin' on You" helped put
Mars on the map as an artist.

CHAPTER 6

Hitting the Road

||||||||||||||||||||||||||

Mars was universally praised for his work as a songwriter and a featured guest on successful songs such as "Nothin' On You" and "Billionaire." Back when he was still an artist in search of a label, record companies had complained his style was too hard to pin down. Now they were praising his musical versatility. Eventually, Elektra Records, part of Atlantic Records, signed Mars as a solo

"Billionaire," Mars's collaboration with Travie McCoy, *right*, peaked at Number 4 on the *Billboard* Hot 100.

artist in 2009. "He's just so talented," said John Janick, who was copresident of Elektra at the time. "The rock alternative bands think he's amazing, he has these pop hits and mass culture likes him, he's got this rhythm-urban feel to him, and he can go into any of those worlds and make great-sounding songs."[1]

"He's got a really refreshing and effortless voice," said Travie McCoy, who recorded "Billionaire" with Mars. "And this dude could write a hit record sitting on the toilet," said McCoy. "He's just got it in him."[2]

IT'S BETTER IF YOU DON'T UNDERSTAND

Mars had a lot of hit records in him. But in May 2010, his record company didn't want him to rush into recording a whole album. Instead, he released a four-track EP, or extended-play recording, titled *It's Better If You Don't Understand*. Atlantic/Elektra wanted Mars to take his time and pull together a bigger collection of songs for a future album. "We felt like [the EP] would be the right introductory piece and a good strategy," Janick said.[3]

The first track on *It's Better If You Don't Understand,* "Somewhere in Brooklyn," is a snappy, catchy electro-pop song about losing a girl. For "The Other Side," Mars reunited with his former collaborators Cee Lo Green and B.o.B. "Count on Me" is another upbeat tune, in which he tells the object of his affection, "If you ever find yourself lost in the dark and you can't see, I'll be the light to guide you."[4] Rounding out the four-track album is a romantic piano ballad called "Talking to the Moon."

Even with the short EP, Mars conveyed many human emotions in its four tracks. "Mars's songs connect to our common elements of humanity," said Atlantic Records executive vice president Andrea Ganis. "Love, acceptance, loss. The ability to marry those sentiments to engaging melodies is what makes his appeal so broad."[5]

> **"I want my songs to just kind of smack you . . . I don't overthink it. I'm not a poetic guy."[7]**
>
> —*BRUNO MARS*

ON TOUR

In 2010, Mars started a tour to promote his new songs. He had offers to play in large concert halls opening for big music acts, but he decided to perform in small concert venues instead. Mars chose a smaller setting because he wanted a chance to get to know his fans, saying:

> *I love the feeling I get when I'm on stage and I can see people dancing to the music we're playing and I can see smiles and I can see someone's eyes and I can let them know, "I see you."*[6]

Bruno's unusual venue choices were based on a long-term strategy, not immediate financial gain, according to Randy Phillips, CEO of AEG, a concert promotion company. "He chose to play smaller venues to build his fan base and grow his career, and I respect him for that."[8] "As a new artist," Mars said, "it's important to show the core fans what I sound like live . . . for them to hear every single line and see the intricacy that we all put into a show."[9]

BOWERY BALLROOM

One of the small, intimate venues where Bruno Mars played during his early tour was the Bowery Ballroom in New York. On August 25, 2010, the 24-year-old Mars performed his first solo show at the Bowery in front of a sold-out crowd. The band wore matching blue blazers and skinny ties and featured his writing-producing partner, Lawrence, performing backup vocals and Mars's brother, Eric, on drums.

Because he had been performing for most of his life, Mars was totally at ease on stage. "He was a natural showman, as if he'd been doing it for decades," one reporter wrote.[10] But this performance was also different from his early Elvis impersonations and renditions of doo-wop classics. "It was the first time I was singing my songs and the crowd was singing them back," Mars said.[11]

TROUBLE WITH THE LAW

Mars's career was finally on the right path. His music was getting a lot of attention. By the fall of 2010, he was one of the hottest young performers in the music industry. Suddenly, though, Mars found himself in trouble with the law.

On September 19, 2010, 24-year-old Mars was performing at the Hard Rock Hotel & Casino in Las Vegas, Nevada. After the show, he went into a bathroom stall. Hotel security found him there with 0.09 ounces (2.6 g) of cocaine. Police officers soon arrived and arrested Mars.

Mars felt horrible about the incident. "I was embarrassed. It was me being extremely, extremely careless, and not thinking," he said.[12] He pleaded guilty and received probation rather than jail

"It's all about . . . putting on a show. I think the best part of our show is that you can tell that we're all friends up there . . . We go up there and genuinely have the time of our life. And I think that's . . . what makes the audience just want to get involved."[13]

—BRUNO MARS

Mars's relatively clean image hit a snag with his Las Vegas arrest for cocaine possession.

time. He paid a $2,000 fine, did 200 hours of community service, and saw a drug counselor.

Afterward, Mars tried to put the incident behind him, but celebrity tabloids continued to cover the story. The media didn't want to stop writing—or talking—about the arrest. Bruno said, "It's a cloud that constantly follows me . . . I'd like to move on. To show that I'm here for my music. Not to be in a tabloid."[14]

COMING HOME

Mars helped himself move on from the arrest by going home. In December 2010, he boarded a plane and headed back to Honolulu. Just a few years earlier, when he was broke in Los Angeles, he was on the verge of giving up on his recording career and moving back there for good. Now he was returning to his birthplace as a famous singer-songwriter with several hit singles.

Instead of playing in hotel lounges like he'd done when he was a teenager, Mars headlined a sold-out show at the Blaisdell Arena in Waikiki.

MARS'S GUITARS

Some people name their cars or their homes. Bruno Mars names his guitars. Most of those guitars are Fenders, the iconic brand created by California inventor Leo Fender in the 1940s. Music legends such as Jimi Hendrix, Eric Clapton, and Jeff Beck have all played Fender guitars. Bruno Mars has a Fender precision bass named Bophus Leon and one called Red Sasha. He also has a Fender Stratocaster, which he named Erika.

As he walked to the stage on the night of December 19, the crowd of approximately 10,000 people began chanting, "Bruno! Bruno! Bruno!"[15] When he appeared on stage, they let out an ear-splitting scream.

As the former "world's youngest Elvis," it was fitting Mars started his show with the opening from the movie *2001: A Space Odyssey*. Elvis was introduced to the stage the same way during his 1973 "Aloha From Hawaii" concert at the Blaisdell Arena. "For Bruno the evening was a triumphant homecoming," one reviewer wrote.[16]

One of the biggest moments in the show came before Mars even stepped out onto the stage. His father's band, the Love Notes, opened for Mars with a doo-wop performance. Peter Hernandez was thrilled to be back on the same stage with his now famous son. Hernandez said,

I was blown away by him—truly in awe. His professionalism was so polished and so sharp. As much as I love performing, I felt that if I never did another show in my life, I would be content.[17]

||||||||||

Mars performed at the Grammy Nominations Concert in December 2010.

CHAPTER 7

Doo-Wops & Hooligans

||||||||||||||||||||||||||||||||||||||||||||||||||||

Bruno Mars and the Smeezingtons spent three years writing songs. By 2010, they had compiled more than enough music to make an entire album. They recorded the album at Levcon Studios and put the finishing touches on it at Larrabee Studios in North Hollywood. Mars and the Smeezingtons worked with legendary producer Manny Marroquin. The five-time Grammy Award winner

Bruno Mars and the Smeezingtons do much of their recording at a small Los Angeles studio called Levcon. Ari Levine coowns the studio with his manager and brother, Josh.

For the Smeezingtons, the process of writing a song starts with the musicians playing something freestyle until a song begins to take shape. Mars might play guitar and piano, while Levine adds the drum track and Lawrence sings. Writing and recording an entire album is an exhausting process that can take months—or even years. When they are in the middle of recording, they often spend long hours in the studio. "I'm here from when I wake up to when I go to sleep, about six days a week," Mars said.[1]

With a couple of hit records under their belts, the Smeezingtons could have moved to a bigger studio. But they decided to stay at Levcon. "[W]e always find that we still do our best work in our little shack of a studio," Lawrence said. "That's where we find our magic."[2]

had already helped produce hits for artists such as Alicia Keys, Rihanna, and Usher. Could he do the same for Mars?

The ten songs Mars recorded combined a variety of musical genres, including pop, rock, and 1960s R&B. On October 5, 2010, Mars released his debut full-length album, *Doo-Wops & Hooligans*.

It debuted at Number 3 on the *Billboard* Top 40 chart.

Doo-Wops & Hooligans spun off three monster hits. "The Lazy Song" is Mars's tribute to doing absolutely nothing. In "Just the Way You Are," Mars reassures his girl that she is amazing exactly the way she is. And "Grenade" is about his willingness to do anything—even catch a

MERCHANDISING

Once a musician becomes famous, his or her income rises exponentially. Artists don't make money just by selling CDs and concert tickets. They also put their name and face on everything from T-shirts to mouse pads to coffee mugs.

When Bruno Mars became a star, he put his name on one very memorable item. The idea for the product in question came from "The Lazy Song," in which he sings, "I'll be loungin' on the couch just chillin' in my Snuggie."[3] A Snuggie is a sleeved, body-length blanket. Not long after the song was released, a similar blanket bearing Mars's signature went on sale on his Web site. The Bruno Mars Snuggie is no longer for sale, but Mars still sells T-shirts and CDs on his Web site. Mars sells merchandise like other artists, but swears he will never sell out and promote a bunch of products just for the money. "I'm not going to just take every dollar that's offered, it has to fit right with my brand," he said. "It has to be something I strongly believe in."[4]

grenade—for the woman he loves. The song was inspired by his love for a girl who did not love him back. "I was a bit of a drama queen in that song," he said. "It was therapy."[5] Both "Just the Way You Are" and "Grenade" rose to the top of the music charts. Mars became the first male solo artist to hit Number 1 with his first two singles.

Rolling Stone magazine reviewer Jody Rosen called *Doo-Wops & Hooligans* "the year's finest pop debut: 10 near-perfect songs that move from power ballads to bedroom anthems to pop-reggae and deliver pleasure without [boasting]."[6] The reviewer also called the 25-year-old singer "a lavishly gifted melodist" and "an engaging singer."[7]

All three of the album's singles streaked up the charts. "Just the Way You Are" spent four weeks at Number 1 on the *Billboard* Hot 100 chart and sold 4.5 million copies. "Grenade" hit Number 1 and sold 4.4 million copies in the United States. "The Lazy Song" was downloaded 2 million times. *Doo-Wops & Hooligans* was also a huge hit in other parts of the world, especially in the United Kingdom, Canada, Germany, and Ireland.

Mars with his 2011 Grammy for Best Male Pop Vocal Performance

After the album was released, Mars went on tour to support it—this time playing in much larger venues with Maroon 5 and Travie McCoy. Then he launched the Doo-Wops & Hooligans Tour and later coheadlined shows with R&B singer Janelle Monáe. They became friends and there were even rumors of a romantic relationship, which Monáe quickly denied. "He's like a little brother," she said. "Everyone wants to see us date. It's so funny."[8]

RECOGNITION

On February 13, 2011, Mars celebrated his newfound success at the Grammy Awards, considered the highest honor in the music industry. After years of collaborating, Mars was recognized with seven Grammy nominations. Mars and the Smeezingtons were nominated for Producer of the Year, Non-Classical. "Nothin' On You" was nominated for Record of the Year, Best Rap/Sung Collaboration, and Best Rap Song. "[Forget] You," his collaboration with Cee Lo Green, was nominated for both Record of the Year and Song of the Year. But it was Mars's performance as a solo artist that won him a trophy.

WHERE MARS KEEPS HIS GRAMMY

Winning a Grammy Award in 2011 was one of the highlights of Bruno Mars's career. So where does he keep this coveted award? "I move it around the house," he said. "Right now it's in my office, next to an award for Outstanding Wedding Band I was given three or four years ago."[9]

He took home a Grammy for Best Male Pop Vocal Performance for "Just The Way You Are."

During the show, Mars also performed a doo-wop version of his single "Grenade." He wore a suit and tie and was backed by a trio of singers. The performance inspired one reviewer to write, "At this point, it's no surprise that Bruno Mars can put on a good show, but his Grammy performance . . . was a total blast."[10]

MARS'S CRITICS

As his songs rose up the charts, Mars enjoyed almost universal praise from fans. But some critics were not always so positive about his work. Mike Diver, an online reviewer for the British Broadcasting Company (BBC) called *Doo-Wops & Hooligans* "some of the most uninspired music one might stumble across in 2011."[11]

Just about every musician faces criticism sometimes. And every musician handles bad reviews differently. When critics lashed out at Mars's work, he hit right back. "*You* write a song then. That's how I feel," he said to *CBS Sunday*

Morning.[12] Mars is perfectly happy with the kind of music he performs. "I am what I am," he said. "I know that 'Just the Way You Are' is not a Sex Pistols [a 1970s punk band] record. That's what it is, it's for the masses. And I'm totally happy with that."[13]

Despite some bad responses to his music, Mars was on top of the world. In September 2010, he sang for a group of approximately 150 fans at Waterloo Records shop in Austin, Texas. After the miniconcert, he was asked how he felt. "I'm happy now," he said.[14]

||||||||||

Despite some criticism, by
2011 Mars had achieved success
with his own solo album.

Mars didn't stop with the success of *Doo-Wops & Hooligans.*

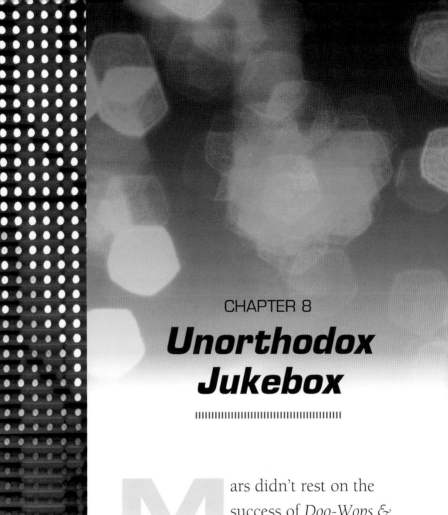

CHAPTER 8

Unorthodox Jukebox

|||||||||||||||||||||||||||||||||||||||||||||||

Mars didn't rest on the success of *Doo-Wops & Hooligans*. Soon after its release, he was ready to get back into the studio and record his second album. "I feel like you have to constantly keep proving yourself, and you have to constantly keep getting out there and showing them you're more than just that one song on the radio that's just playing," he said.[1]

In late 2011, Mars started working on his second album, *Unorthodox Jukebox*. He invited a dream team of his favorite producers into the Levcon recording studio. They included producers Diplo and Paul Epworth. Epworth cowrote the song "Rolling in the Deep" with British singer-songwriter Adele. Mars also recruited former Sex Panther Bhasker, who had worked with Mars on *Doo-Wops & Hooligans*. Bhasker had also collaborated with other artists such as Adam Lambert, Beyoncé, and Fun.

> **"I want to have the freedom and luxury to walk into a studio and say, 'Today I want to do a hip-hop, R&B, soul or rock record.'"[2]**
>
> —*BRUNO MARS*

Mars also brought in producer Mark Ronson. He loved the creative and diverse production work Ronson had done for singer Amy Winehouse's 2007 album *Back to Black*, which won five Grammy Awards. "You couldn't put it in a box 'cause it could be played on rhythmic stations, it could be played on pop radio, and I've always wanted to make music like that—that could be spread out, and can't be pigeon-held [sic] to one thing," Mars said.[3]

Ronson got the call to take part in the *Unorthodox Jukebox* recording session when he was on his honeymoon in the Zanzibar Archipelago off the coast of East Africa. "I was only kind of familiar with his music, but we met up in London a month later and he won me over," Ronson said. "I found out what a phenomenal talent he is."[4]

||||||||||||||||||||||||||||||||||||||||||||||||||||||||||||||

MORE RECOGNITION

While hard at work on his second album, Mars's first effort as a solo artist continued to receive recognition. He won Top Radio Song for "Just the Way You Are" at the *Billboard* Music Awards in May 2011 and Favorite Pop/Rock Male Artist at the American Music Awards in November 2011.

In December 2011, Mars received six 2012 Grammy nominations. *Doo-Wops & Hooligans* was nominated for both Best Pop Vocal Album and Album of the Year. "Grenade" received nominations for Best Pop Solo Performance,

Mars was praised for his performance at the 2012 Grammys.

Song of the Year, and Record of the Year. Mars was grateful for the nominations, particularly for "Grenade," because "that's the song we worked the hardest [on]. Most proud of that one."[5]

At the ceremony on February 12, 2012, Mars ended up losing to Adele in each of his categories. But he still put on a great show, performing his song "Runaway Baby" in a gold blazer and bow tie with a full band behind him. During his performance, Mars paid tribute to singer

Whitney Houston, who had died the night before the ceremony. "We celebrate the beautiful Miss Whitney Houston," he said.[6]

Mars appeared to channel the spirit of 1960s soul musician James Brown, who was known as the Godfather of Soul. Mars danced around the stage with movements similar to Brown's. Mars then dropped into a half-split, one of Brown's signature moves. At the end of the performance, Mars got a standing ovation. MTV described it as a "dazzling performance," saying, "Mars lifted the mood in the room."[7]

MUSICAL MIX

Of course, Mars's writing-producing trio, the Smeezingtons, was a major part of *Unorthodox Jukebox*'s production. Mars and the rest of his team spent six months holed up in the studio, trying to get the new album just right. Sometimes Mars stayed there around the clock. He expected nothing less than perfection on each song. "I've never seen someone be so meticulous in my entire life, when it comes to anything," said Ari Levine.[8]

Mars has made countless promotional appearances since his career took off in 2010.

It took three months just to write a second verse for the song "Moonshine."

Although Elektra Records released *Doo-Wops & Hooligans*, record executives felt Atlantic Records, also owned by Warner Music Group, was a better fit for *Unorthodox Jukebox*. *Unorthodox Jukebox* was Mars's chance to write and record any style of music he wanted. "With this album, I wanna let loose," he said.[9] And that's just what he did, especially after Atlantic gave him complete artistic freedom. "Our relationship with them has been incredible," Mars said.[10]

The Smeezingtons and their collaborators did not write music before they went into the recording session. They wrote as they jammed. Bhasker played the keyboard, Ronson hit the electronic drums, and Mars sang until some of the album's songs began to form. "We took some master chefs into the kitchen with no master plan," said Mars. "It was either going to be a disaster, or we were going to come out with something incredible."[11]

Unorthodox Jukebox was an album filled with different musical inspirations—from old-fashioned R&B to 1980s New Wave. It included everything from piano ballads to funk, pop, doo-wop, and reggae. Each song has its own sound. The song "Locked Out of Heaven" sounds similar to music by the Police, a 1980s English rock band, while "Moonshine" has a more discolike groove. "Gorilla" starts with a rhythmic, thumping jungle beat with hard-rock guitars wailing underneath. Many of the songs are a lot edgier than anything Mars had recorded before.

"Locked Out of Heaven" was the first song from the album to be released, making its digital and radio debut on October 1, 2012.

On September 19, 2012, Mars announced the completion of his second album, *Unorthodox Jukebox*, via the social media Web site Twitter. In the announcement to his 12 million followers, Mars also included a link to the Web site, Funny or Die. It was a parody featuring Mars set to "Whatta Man," a 1994 song by hip-hop trio Salt-n-Pepa. In the funny video, Mars displayed his versatility and sense of humor. He pretends to be a gunslinger, a dancer in gold hot pants, a smooth spy character, the "Bruno" Paper Towel Man, and a karate master. He even rescues a dog from a burning building and delivers a baby.

The entire *Unorthodox Jukebox* album was released in December.

Mars was already one of the biggest selling artists in the country. His last album had sold more than 5 million copies, and it had spun off 45 million single sales worldwide. Critics felt *Unorthodox Jukebox* sounded similar in many ways to his first album. But this time, Mars reveals a more mature side. The album explores themes such as sex and anger.

Reviews for the album were mixed, even though most critics praised Mars's talent. "Not everything on the new album is brilliant . . . At times it seems his skills as a composer might not be as fully developed as his wickedly expressive singing," wrote Tom Moon from National Public Radio (NPR). But, Moon continued, "it's clear that Mars has crazy potential."[12] *Entertainment Weekly* reviewer Melissa Maerz wrote, "His talent for crafting little pop perfections of all stripes is undeniable."[13]

TOURS AND *SATURDAY NIGHT LIVE*

Mars promoted *Unorthodox Jukebox* by making the rounds both on television shows and in concert halls. On October 20, 2012, Mars appeared on the late-night sketch comedy show *Saturday Night Live*. Mars was not only the musical guest, he was also the host. His appearance showed off his knack for comedy and celebrity impersonations. Mars helped earn *Saturday Night Live* one of the show's highest episodes during the 2012–2013 season. The *Huffington Post* said he "stole the show."[14]

In February 2013, Mars announced the launch of his five-month Moonshine Jungle Tour. Starting in June 2013, the tour sent Mars throughout North America, Europe, and Australia. Mars wanted the songs he wrote for his album to be performed live. "He's such a killer performer and loves being on the road," said Julie Greenwald, chairman and

MARS'S SILLY SIDE

Mars is well known for his sense of humor, as well as his music. He has been known to suddenly break into a silly song or start talking like actor Joe Pesci, an Italian-American known for his roles in mob movies such as *GoodFellas*. "He works to put everyone around him at ease, dishing out compliments or, just as often, gently ribbing," Jonah Weiner of *Rolling Stone* wrote.[15]

That humor was on full display when he hosted *Saturday Night Live*. In one skit, Mars played a Pandora Internet Radio intern named Devin. When the power went out at the radio station, Devin had to sing the vocals for songs on his versatility, Mars did spot-on impersonations of singers such as Michael Jackson, Steven Tyler, Katy Perry, Justin Bieber, and Louis Armstrong. Mars also played a desk clerk wearing an eye patch at a wilderness lodge and a lonely guy who gets a job wearing a mouse suit in Times Square in New York City.

Mars even dressed up in drag to play a 17-year-old girl on a trashy talk show called *Haters*. His character told the audience, "You just jealous because I'm young and I got a debit card and I know where the paa-rty is."[16] Mars said he was able to capture the essence of a teenage girl so well because "I've dated girls like that."[17]

Chief Operating Officer (COO) of Atlantic Records. "He needed an album that he wants to be out on the road with 365 nights performing. That's what this album is."[18]

|||||||||||||||||||||||||||||||||||||||||||||||||||||||||||||

RELATIONSHIPS

Someone with Mars's voice and looks is bound to attract some female admirers. During Mars's onstage performances, his female fans commonly greet him with screams of excitement. Mars has dated many women in the past, but he has never been very public about his personal relationships. He is very quiet about his personal life. Whenever Mars was asked who he was dating, he avoided the question. Once, he joked to a reporter that he was dating actress Halle Berry. He wasn't.

Mars has not been entirely able to hide his private life, though. The media has linked him to a few women over the years, including actress Chanel Malvar and singer Janelle Monaé. Mars has maintained he and Monaé were just friends. In 2009, Mars was hired to write songs for British singer Rita Ora. The two soon started dating. But in 2011, both Ora and Mars had growing careers.

Mars was dating model and actress Jessica Caban as of August 2013.

With work getting in the way, the two ended their relationship.

Later in 2011, Mars was more open about a new relationship with 29-year-old model and actress Jessica Caban. Caban appeared in Mars's "Whatta Man" video on the comedy Web site Funny or Die. Mars reportedly wrote the song "When I Was Your Man" on *Unorthodox Jukebox* when he feared a breakup with Caban because he had not done enough to keep her happy. In the song, Mars sings, "I should've bought you flowers and held your hand."[19]

In 2012, Caban moved into Mars's Hollywood mansion. The pair vacationed together in Hawaii, where Mars reportedly introduced Caban to his mother. "I feel like I'm blessed to have someone to enjoy things with," Mars has said about Caban.[20] Mars has talked about marriage and having children, but the couple was not engaged as of August 2013.

||||||||||

Mars performed in Northern Ireland in May 2013.

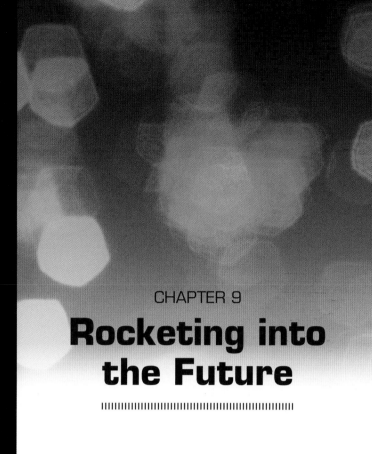

CHAPTER 9

Rocketing into the Future

||||||||||||||||||||||||||||||||||||||||||||||||||||||||

By the spring of 2013, Mars's career was on a high note. His two albums, *Doo-Wops & Hooligans* and *Unorthodox Jukebox*, had together sold approximately 9 million copies around the world. He'd had four Number 1 hits, as well as several other chart-topping singles. His videos had been seen online 1.5 billion times as of May 2013. And, he was about to launch the Moonshine Jungle Tour, which

Mars is probably the dream prom date for a lot of his teenage female fans. But one high school student actually had enough guts to ask him. In December 2012, 16-year-old Emily Torres from Port Huron, Michigan, made a YouTube video inviting Mars to her junior prom. Unfortunately, Mars could not make the prom in March 2013. But he surprised Torres with a dance on *The Ellen DeGeneres Show* in February 2013. During the interview, Mars quickly snapped on a tux and Torres changed into a dress. The two danced to the song "Always and Forever" by Heatwave. Mars also gave her a $4,500 Gucci gown to wear to her prom. After the prom, Torres auctioned off the dress for charity. She gave all the proceeds to a friend who was battling cancer.

would take him across the United States, as well as to Europe, Canada, and Australia.

At just 27 years old, Mars had conquered the music industry. He was able to discredit every record company executive who had said someone who looked and sounded as unique as he did couldn't make it in the music industry.

Mars also accomplished something few musicians can do. He created music that appealed to every audience, young and old. "You go to a Bruno Mars show and you'll see plenty of

8-year-old kids and plenty of grandparents bringing their grandkids. It's really a show for everyone," said Aaron Bay-Schuck Atlantic Records senior vice president of A&R.[1]

||||||||||||||||||||||||||||||||||||||||||||||||||||||||

MORE COLLABORATIONS

Mars had started his career writing songs for other singers such as Cee Lo Green and B.o.B. Once he became successful as a solo artist, he didn't have to

GIVING BACK ||||||||||||||||||||||||||||||||||||||||||||||||||||||||||||||||||||||||||||||||||||||||||||||||||

After achieving success in the music industry, Mars has tried to share his good fortune with others. Mars closely supports m.a.m.a. earth, a charity started by his sister Jaime. The organization hosts music, art, and nature events and classes and supports local and global causes. Whenever he is available, Mars performs at m.a.m.a. earth events or provides video messages and autographed Fender guitars.

Mars has also performed at events for several other charities, including the Global Poverty Project, the EIF Women's Cancer Research Fund, and Artists Project Earth. Joining a group of celebrities, in January 2012, Mars provided his musical talents at Hilarity for Charity, an event to help raise money and awareness for Alzheimer's disease.

At the 2013 Grammys, Mars performed with singer Sting, *left,* in a tribute to musician Bob Marley.

write for anyone. But he still enjoyed collaborating with other musicians.

In 2012, Mars wrote the song "Tears Always Win" for R&B singer Alicia Keys's album *Girl On Fire.* He said it had always been his dream to work with Keys. He was featured on the "Lighters," with rappers Eminem and Royce da 5'9". Mars has said he still wants to work with several other artists, including Kanye West, Jay Z, Rihanna, Lady Gaga, and the Kings of Leon. One day, Mars hopes to discover a new talent. "My goal is to find a new artist; I'd love to produce a whole album that I'm not singing on," he said.[2]

FRUITS OF HIS SUCCESS

To celebrate his success, Mars bought himself a $3.3 million mansion in the Hollywood Hills in 2012. The 4,061-square-foot (377 sq m) single-floor home has three bedrooms and three and a half bathrooms. It also has a media room, pool, sauna, and parking for ten cars. The house might sound rich, but by pop star standards, it's not very extravagant. In spite of his money and fame, Mars still considers himself a simple guy. "I don't throw lavish parties or nothing like that, I just want a bed and a TV," Mars said.[3]

To make his home complete, Mars's girlfriend, Jessica Caban, moved in with him. He also got a dog—a Rottweiler named Geronimo. Behind the sofa hang three posters from Elvis's movies *King Creole* (1958), *Blue Hawaii* (1961), and *Girls! Girls! Girls!* (1962), which used to belong to Mars's father.

Mars also put some of his earnings into the purchase of a big black Cadillac with tinted windows. Like Mars, his car is a throwback to an earlier era. As one reporter said, "Mars is an old-fashioned kind of pop star, a dimpled, sharp-dressed, elastic-voiced, lady-charming showman who would've been just as successful circa 1960."[4]

LOOKING TOWARD THE FUTURE

Mars has been asked whether he will take on other types of projects, such as acting. Many other musicians have crossed over into acting, including Prince in *Purple Rain* (1984), Eminem in *8 Mile* (2002), and singer Justin Timberlake in *The Social Network* (2010). Mars said he had fun acting on *Saturday Night Live* and he loves *Purple Rain*. But he does not consider himself to be an actor and would have to find a role he really wanted before agreeing to star in a movie. "If there's something that I really feel like, 'Man, no one could do this but me; this is a challenge that I could sink my teeth into,' then I'd give it a shot, definitely. But that's not what the goal is," Mars told one reporter.[5]

Mars doesn't know exactly what the future holds for him, but music will be a part of it. He told *Rolling Stone* magazine:

In 2013, everything was looking up for Mars. But on June 1, 2013, the unthinkable happened when Bernadette, Mars's 55-year-old mother, died suddenly in Honolulu. Her death was caused by a brain aneurysm, a balloonlike bulge in one of her brain's blood vessels. It was a difficult time for her family, including Mars. He had been very close to his mother. Media reports of Bernadette's death included a heartwarming recording of a four-year-old Mars singing a song he'd written for his mother: "I love you Mom. You are my favorite girl."[7] Close to a week after his mother's shocking death, Mars expressed his gratitude for the support of fans. "So thankful for all the love during the most difficult time in my life. Ill [sic] be back on my feet again soon. Thats [sic] what mom wants, she told me," Mars wrote.[8]

I don't know where I'm gonna end up. But I want to keep writing songs, man. There's a feeling you get from writing a good song that you don't get from anything else. You forever want that feeling, the same way you forever want to eat good food, you forever want to be in love.[6]

Atlantic Records chairman and COO Julie Greenwald believes Mars will get exactly what he wants out of his career. "It's definitely not going to be a case of here today, gone tomorrow," she said.

With credits as a singer, songwriter, and producer, Mars has established a successful career at a young age.

"This is a guy who's going to be doing this for the next 50 years. His commitment to performing, touring, and creating is so real and so genuine that nothing is going to knock him off."[9]

"I feel like, 'Oh, man. People haven't seen nothing. They don't even know what I'm about to do,' and that's what I can't wait to show the world."[12]

—*BRUNO MARS*

Bruno Mars has no plans to leave the music business anytime soon. Even when he thinks ahead, retirement seems hard to imagine. "Hopefully in ten years, I'll be on a beach somewhere, getting a phone call about a reunion tour with the boys," he joked. "Of course I'll be overweight, and singing the songs about four keys lower."[10] But Mars says he hopes to stay just the way he is, "creating the kind of music that I want to create. And if I'm lucky, I'll have taken a lot of people on that journey with me."[11]

||||||||||

TIMELINE

1985

Bruno Mars is born on October 8 in Honolulu, Hawaii.

1992

Bruno has a cameo as Little Elvis in the movie *Honeymoon in Vegas*.

2004

Mars signs a $100,000 recording contract with Universal Motown Records.

2009

"Right Round" is released and becomes Mars's first songwriting hit.

2009

Mars signs a recording contract with Elektra Records.

2010

Mars cowrites "[Forget] You" with singer Cee Lo Green, which reaches Number 2 on the *Billboard* Hot 100.

2005	**2005**	**2005**
Mars is dropped from his record label without releasing an album.	Mars starts the band Sex Panther with his brother, Eric, and Jeff Bhasker.	Mars forms the songwriting-producing team, the Smeezingtons.

2010	**2010**	**2010**
Mars collaborates on hit songs "Nothin' On You" with rapper B.o.B. and "Billionaire" with Travie McCoy.	In May, Mars releases his first EP, *It's Better If You Don't Understand*.	Mars is arrested for drug possession at the Hard Rock Hotel & Casino in Las Vegas, Nevada, on September 19.

TIMELINE

2010

On October 5, Mars releases his first full-length album, *Doo-Wops & Hooligans*.

2010

In December, Mars goes home to perform a sold-out concert at the Blaisdell Arena in Waikiki, Hawaii.

2010

Mars is nominated for seven Grammy Awards.

2011

Mars wins Favorite Pop/ Rock Male Artist at the American Music Awards in November.

2012

Mars hosts and performs on *Saturday Night Live* on October 20.

2012

Mars's second album, *Unorthodox Jukebox*, is released on December 11.

2010

"Grenade" reaches Number 1 on the *Billboard* Hot 100 chart.

2011

Mars wins the Grammy for Best Male Pop Vocal Performance for "Just the Way You Are" in February.

2011

In May, Mars wins Top Radio Song for "Just the Way You Are" at the *Billboard* Music Awards.

2012

Mars performs at the 54th Grammy Awards on February 12.

2013

Mars's mother, Bernadette, passes away on June 1.

2013

Mars launches his Moonshine Jungle Tour in June.

GET THE SCOOP

FULL NAME

Peter Gene Hernandez Jr.

DATE OF BIRTH

October 8, 1985

PLACE OF BIRTH

Honolulu, Hawaii

ALBUMS

It's Better If You Don't Understand EP (2010), *Doo-Wops & Hooligans* (2010), *Unorthodox Jukebox* (2012)

TOURS

Doo-Wops & Hooligans Tour (2010–2012), Moonshine Jungle Tour (2013)

SELECTED AWARDS

- Won the 2011 Grammy Award for Best Male Pop Vocal Performance of "Just the Way You Are."
- Won the 2011 American Music Award for Favorite Pop/Rock Male Artist.
- Won the 2011 *Billboard* Music Award for Top Radio Song for "Just the Way You Are."

PHILANTHROPY

Mars supports m.a.m.a. earth, a charity started by his sister Jaime, which hosts music, art, and nature events in support of local and global causes. He provides signed Fender guitars for auction and performs at events hosted by the charity. Mars has also performed at other charitable events, including Hilarity for Charity, which helps raise money and awareness for Alzheimer's disease.

"I don't know where I'm gonna end up. But I want to keep writing songs, man. There's a feeling you get from writing a good song that you don't get from anything else. You forever want that feeling, the same way you forever want to eat good food, you forever want to be in love."

—BRUNO MARS

GLOSSARY

a cappella—Without the accompaniment of music.

bell-bottoms—A type of jeans worn in the 1970s with wide, flared legs at the bottom.

Billboard—A music chart system used by the music recording industry to measure record popularity or sales.

chart—A weekly listing of songs or albums in order of popularity or record sales.

collaborate—To work together in order to create or produce a work, such as a song or album.

demo—An initial recording meant to demonstrate a musician's talent to a record producer.

EP—Extended play, a type of record that contains more than one song, but does not have enough songs to be called a full album.

fedora—A soft felt hat creased along the length of its brim.

freestyle—To perform verses on the spot rather than using prewritten lyrics.

genre—A category of art, music, or literature characterized by a particular style, form, or content.

Grammy Award—One of several awards the National Academy of Recording Arts and Sciences presents each year to honor musical achievement.

hip-hop—A style of popular music associated with American urban culture that features rap spoken against a background of electronic music beats.

pompadour—A type of men's hairstyle from the 1950s in which the hair is combed up high on the head.

probation—The release of someone from prison under the terms they will behave and will continue to be supervised.

producer—Someone who oversees or provides money for a play, television show, movie, or album.

revue—A type of show that features singing, dancing, and sometimes comedy or acting.

rhythm and blues—A kind of music that—especially in modern times—typically combines hip-hop, soul, and funk.

studio—A room with electronic recording equipment where music, television, or film is recorded.

tabloid—A newspaper or magazine that publishes sensational stories, often about celebrities.

venue—The place where a concert or other event is held.

versatility—Having a variety of skills in many different areas.

ADDITIONAL RESOURCES

SELECTED BIBLIOGRAPHY

Greenburg, Zack O'Malley. "Mars Attacks!" *Forbes*. Forbes, 6 June 2011. Web. 20 Apr. 2013.

Heath, Chris. "The Mars Expedition." *GQ*. Condé Nast, Apr. 2013. Web. 20 Apr. 2013.

Vozick-Levinson, Simon and Karen Valby. "Bruno Mars Triumph & Trouble." *Entertainment Weekly*. Entertainment Weekly, 24 Sept. 2010. Web. 20 Apr. 2013.

FURTHER READINGS

Cowlin, Chris. *The Bruno Mars Quiz Book*. Essex, England: Apex Publishing Ltd., 2011. E-book.

Smith, Bieber J. *Bruno Mars – Biography of a Pop Star*. Amazon Digital Services, Inc., 2012. E-book.

Watson, Stephanie. *Elvis Presley: Rock & Roll's King*. Minneapolis: ABDO, 2012. Print.

WEB SITES

To learn more about Bruno Mars, visit ABDO Publishing Company online at **www.abdopublishing.com**. Web sites about Bruno Mars are featured on our Book Links page. These links are routinely monitored and updated to provide the most current information available.

PLACES TO VISIT

Graceland

3734 Elvis Presley Boulevard, Memphis, TN 38116
901-332-3329
http://www.elvis.com/graceland
Graceland was the home of the King of Rock & Roll and Mars's earliest influence, Elvis Presley.

Hawaii Visitors and Convention Bureau

2270 Kalakaua Avenue, Suite 801, Honolulu, HI 96815
1-800-464-2924
http://www.gohawaii.com
Visit this tropical paradise and Mars's birthplace.

SOURCE NOTES

CHAPTER 1. NEW YORK CITY IS ON MARS

1. Richard Smirke. "Pop Matters." *Billboard* 23 July 2011: 21. Print.
2. "Z100 Jingle Ball 2010 Bruno Mars Intro." *YouTube*. YouTube, 11 Dec. 2010. Web. 25 May 2013.
3. Ibid.
4. Richard Smirke. "Pop Matters." *Billboard* 23 July 2011: 22. Print.
5. Ibid.
6. Jonah Weiner. "Mr. Showbiz." *Rolling Stone* 20 Jan. 2011: 50. *Zinio Digital Magazines*. Web. 20 Apr. 2013.
7. Ibid.
8. Ibid.
9. Ibid. 51.

CHAPTER 2. THE LITTLEST ELVIS

1. "Bruno Mars." *Biography*. A&E Networks Television, n.d. Web. 20 Apr. 2013.
2. John Berger. "Bruno Mars." *Honolulu Star-Advertiser*. Star-Advertiser, 13 Feb. 2011. Web. 30 Apr. 2013.
3. Ibid.
4. "Bruno Mars." *CBS News*. CBS, 9 Dec. 2012. Web. 24 Apr. 2013.
5. Jonah Weiner. "Mr. Showbiz." *Rolling Stone* 20 Jan. 2011: 50. *Zinio Digital Magazines*. Web. 20 Apr. 2013.
6. Dave Dondoneau. "Bruno Mars Traces Swagger to Elvis Stint in Läie." *Honolulu Advertiser*. Honolulu Advertiser, 14 May 2010. Web. 6 May 2013.
7. Denise Quan. "Bruno Mars Heads for the Stars with New Album." *CNN*. Cable News Network, 5 Oct. 2010. Web. 30 Apr. 2013.
8. Elysa Gardner. "Bruno Mars Goes Back to the Future with 'Jukebox.'" *USA Today*. Gannett, 10 Dec. 2012. Web. 24 July 2013.
9. "Bruno Mars Aged 4." *YouTube*. YouTube, 12 Oct. 2010. Web. 30 Apr. 2013.
10. Jonah Weiner. "Mr. Showbiz." *Rolling Stone* 20 Jan. 2011: 50. *Zinio Digital Magazines*. Web. 20 Apr. 2013.
11. Brian Hiatt. "The Golden Child." *Rolling Stone* 9 May 2013: 42. Print.
12. Austin Scaggs. "Q&A Bruno Mars." *Rolling Stone* 25 Nov. 2010: 34. Print.

CHAPTER 3. LAUNCHING A MUSIC CAREER

1. Austin Scaggs. "Q&A Bruno Mars." *Rolling Stone* 25 Nov. 2010: 34. Print.
2. "Bruno Mars." *CBS News*. CBS, 9 Dec. 2012. Web. 24 Apr. 2013.
3. Brian Hiatt. "The Golden Child." *Rolling Stone* 9 May 2013: 42. Print.
4. "Bruno Mars—Coming Home Documentary." *YouTube*. YouTube, 14 July 2011. Web. 24 Apr. 2013.
5. Caitlin White. "Bruno Mars, Hair." *AOL Music Blog*. AOL Inc., 13 Jan. 2013. Web. 24 July 2013.
6. Jonah Weiner. "Mr. Showbiz." *Rolling Stone* 20 Jan. 2011: 50. *Zinio Digital Magazines*. Web. 20 Apr. 2013.
7. Georgette Cline. "10 Questions for Bruno Mars." *Rap-Up*. Spin Media, 11 May 2010. Web. 24 July 2013.
8. Chris Heath. "The Mars Expedition." *GQ*. Condé Nast, Apr. 2013. Web. 20 Apr. 2013.
9. Simon Vozick-Levinson and Karen Valby. "Bruno Mars Triumph & Trouble." *EW.com*. Entertainment Weekly, 24 Sept. 2010. Web. 20 Apr. 2013.
10. Melissa Moniz. "Starring Bruno Mars." *MidWeek*. MidWeek Printing, 14 Apr. 2010. Web. 7 May 2013.
11. Zack O'Malley Greenburg. "Mars Attacks!" *Forbes*. Forbes, 6 June 2011. Web. 20 Apr. 2013.
12. Chris Heath. "The Mars Expedition." *GQ*. Condé Nast, Apr. 2013. Web. 20 Apr. 2013.

CHAPTER 4. STRUGGLING IN LOS ANGELES

1. Jon Caramanica. "Bruno Mars in Ascension." *New York Times*. New York Times, 5 Oct. 2010. Web. 22 May 2013.

2. Brian Hiatt. "The Golden Child." *Rolling Stone* 9 May 2013: 40. Print.

3. Simon Vozick-Levinson and Karen Valby. "Bruno Mars Triumph & Trouble." *EW.com*. Entertainment Weekly, 24 Sept. 2010. Web. 20 Apr. 2013.

4. "Bruno Mars Grateful for Record Deal Flop." *Contactmusic*. Contactmusic, 24 Jan. 2011. Web. 15 May 2013.

5. Jonah Weiner. "Mr. Showbiz." *Rolling Stone* 20 Jan. 2011: 51. *Zinio Digital Magazines*. Web. 20 Apr. 2013.

6. "Bruno Mars Grateful For Record Deal Flop." *Contactmusic*. Contactmusic, 24 Jan. 2011. Web. 15 May 2013.

7. Brian Hiatt. "The Golden Child." *Rolling Stone* 9 May 2013: 42. Print.

8. Richard Smirke. "Pop Matters." *Billboard* 23 July 2011: 22. Print.

9. Brian Hiatt. "The Golden Child." *Rolling Stone* 9 May 2013: 40. Print.

10. Ibid.

11. "Bruno Mars." *CBS News*. CBS, 9 Dec. 2012. Web. 24 Apr. 2013.

12. "Bruno Mars—Coming Home Documentary." *YouTube*. YouTube, 14 July 2011. Web. 24 Apr. 2013.

CHAPTER 5. FROM SINGER TO SONGWRITER

1. Richard Smirke. "Pop Matters." *Billboard* 23 July 2011: 22. Print.

2. "Lawrence Almost Missed Out on Mars Collaboration." *Contactmusic*. Contactmusic, 22 Feb. 2011. Web. 20 May 2013.

3. Brad Wete. "So Who Is Bruno Mars? *EW.com*. Entertainment Weekly, 13 Apr. 2010. Web. 20 May 2013.

4. Monica Herrera. "Bruno Mars: Stepping Out." *Billboard* 8 May 2010: 30. Print.

5. Dave Dondoneau. "Bruno Mars Traces Swagger to Elvis Stint in Lāie." *Honolulu Advertiser*. Honolulu Advertiser, 14 May 2010. Web. 6 May 2013.

6. Jonah Weiner. "Mr. Showbiz." *Rolling Stone* 20 Jan. 2011: 51. *Zinio Digital Magazines*. Web. 20 Apr. 2013.

7. "Bruno Mars." *CBS News*. CBS, 9 Dec. 2012. Web. 24 Apr. 2013.

8. Matt Diehl. "Caught in Mars' Orbit." *Los Angeles Times*. Los Angeles Times, 6 Feb. 2011. Web. 20 Apr. 2013.

9. Brad Wete. "So Who Is Bruno Mars?" *EW.com*. Entertainment Weekly, 13 Apr. 2010. Web. 20 May 2013.

10. Jonah Weiner. "Mr. Showbiz." *Rolling Stone* 20 Jan. 2011: 51. *Zinio Digital Magazines*. Web. 20 Apr. 2013.

11. Austin Scaggs. "Q&A Bruno Mars." *Rolling Stone* 25 Nov. 2010: 34. Print.

12. Zack O'Malley Greenburg. "Mars Attacks!" *Forbes*. Forbes, 6 June 2011. Web. 20 Apr. 2013.

13. Ibid.

14. "Nothin' On You." *A-Z Lyrics Universe*. AZLyrics.com, n.d. Web. 20 May 2013.

CHAPTER 6. HITTING THE ROAD

1. Zack O'Malley Greenburg. "Mars Attacks!" *Forbes*. Forbes, 6 June 2011. Web. 20 Apr. 2013.

2. Simon Vozick-Levinson and Karen Valby. "Bruno Mars Triumph & Trouble." *EW.com*. Entertainment Weekly, 24 Sept. 2010. Web. 20 Apr. 2013.

3. Monica Herrera. "Bruno Mars: Stepping Out." *Billboard* 8 May 2010: 30. Print.

4. "Bruno Mars—Count on Me." *YouTube*. YouTube, 2 Sept. 2011. Web. 22 May 2013.

5. Richard Smirke. "Pop Matters." *Billboard* 23 July 2011: 23. Print.

6. Leah Greenblatt. "Bruno Mars Is Red Hot." *EW.com*. Entertainment Weekly, 17 May 2013. Web. 24 May 2013.

7. Jonah Weiner. "Mr. Showbiz." *Rolling Stone* 20 Jan. 2011: 51. *Zinio Digital Magazines*. Web. 20 Apr. 2013.

8. Zack O'Malley Greenburg. "Mars Attacks!" *Forbes*. Forbes, 6 June 2011. Web. 20 Apr. 2013.

9. Richard Smirke. "Pop Matters." *Billboard* 23 July 2011: 23. Print.

10. Jon Caramanica. "Bruno Mars in Ascension." *New York Times*. New York Times, 5 Oct. 2010. Web. 22 May 2013.

11. Richard Smirke. "Pop Matters." *Billboard* 23 July 2011: 23. Print.

12. "Bruno Mars." *CBS News*. CBS, 9 Dec. 2012. Web. 24 Apr. 2013.

13. "Bruno Mars—Coming Home Documentary." *YouTube*. YouTube, 14 July 2011. Web. 24 Apr. 2013.

14. Richard Smirke. "Pop Matters." *Billboard* 23 July 2011: 23. Print.

15. "Bruno Mars—Coming Home Documentary." *YouTube*. YouTube, 14 July 2011. Web. 24 Apr. 2013.

16. John Berger. "Review: Bruno Mars at Blaisdell Arena." *Honolulu Pulse*. Star-Advertiser, 20 Dec. 2010. Web. 22 May 2013.

17. John Berger. "Bruno Mars." *Honolulu Star-Advertiser*. Star-Advertiser, 13 Feb. 2011. Web. 30 Apr. 2013.

CHAPTER 7. *DOO-WOPS & HOOLIGANS*

1. Colin Stutz. "The Smeezingtons." *Hollywood Reporter*. Hollywood Reporter, 6 Feb. 2013. Web. 28 May 2013.

2. "Bruno Mars—The Lazy Song." *YouTube*. YouTube, 15 Apr. 2011. Web. 22 May 2013.

3. Zack O'Malley Greenburg. "Mars Attacks!" *Forbes*. Forbes, 6 June 2011. Web. 20 Apr. 2013.

4. Chuck Arnold and Jessica Herndon. "Picks and Pans: Music." *People*. Time, 30 Jan. 2012. Web. 28 May 2013.

5. Jessica Herndon. "Bruno Mars." *People* 30 Jan. 2012: 50. Print.

6. Jody Rosen. "Bruno Mars: Doo-Wops & Hooligans." *Rolling Stone*. Rolling Stone, 5 Oct. 2010. Web. 28 May 2013.

7. Ibid.

8. Christopher Schultz. "Bruno Mars & Janelle Monae Chat Backstage." *Spin*. Spin, 11 May 2011. Web. 28 May 2013.

9. Mitchell Peters. "The Liberation Songs of Bruno Mars." *Billboard*. Prometheus Media, 6 Oct. 2012. Web. 20 Apr. 2013.

10. EW Staff. "Bruno Mars' Grammy Performance"*EW.com*. Entertainment Weekly, 13 Feb. 2011. Web. 28 May 2013.

11. Mike Diver. "BBC Review." *BBC News*. BBC, 20 Jan. 2011. Web. 28 May 2013.

12. "Bruno Mars." *CBS News*. CBS, 9 Dec. 2012. Web. 24 Apr. 2013.

13. Jonah Weiner. "Mr. Showbiz." *Rolling Stone* 20 Jan. 2011: 75. *Zinio Digital Magazines*. Web. 20 Apr. 2013.

14. Simon Vozick-Levinson and Karen Valby. "Bruno Mars Triumph & Trouble." *EW.com*. Entertainment Weekly, 24 Sept. 2010. Web. 20 Apr. 2013.

CHAPTER 8. *UNORTHODOX JUKEBOX*

1. Mesfin Fekadu. "Bruno Mars." *Christian Science Monitor*. Christian Science Monitor, 19 Dec. 2012. Web. 29 May 2013.

2. Mitchell Peters. "The Liberation Songs of Bruno Mars." *Billboard*. Prometheus Media, 6 Oct. 2012. Web. 20 Apr. 2013.

3. Mesfin Fekadu. "Bruno Mars." *Christian Science Monitor*. Christian Science Monitor, 19 Dec. 2012. Web. 29 May 2013.

4. Matt Diehl. "Bruno Mars Recruits Dream Team of Producers for 'Unorthodox Jukebox.'" *Rolling Stone*. Rolling Stone, 13 Nov. 2012. Web. 29 May 2013.

5. Vicki Salemi. "Bruno Mars Lands Six Grammy Nominations." *OK! Magazine*. Odyssey Magazine Publishing Group, 1 Dec. 2011. Web. 27 June 2013.

6. Jocelyn Vena. "Bruno Mars Shines during Grammy Performance." *MTV News*. Viacom, 12 Feb. 2012. Web. 27 June 2013.

7. Ibid.

8. Brian Hiatt. "The Golden Child." *Rolling Stone* 9 May 2013: 42. Print.

9. Matt Diehl. "Bruno Mars Recruits Dream Team of Producers for 'Unorthodox Jukebox.'" *Rolling Stone*. Rolling Stone, 13 Nov. 2012. Web. 29 May 2013.

10. Mitchell Peters. "The Liberation Songs of Bruno Mars." *Billboard*. Prometheus Media, 6 Oct. 2012. Web. 20 Apr. 2013.

11. Matt Diehl. "Bruno Mars Recruits Dream Team of Producers for 'Unorthodox Jukebox.'" *Rolling Stone*. Rolling Stone, 13 Nov. 2012. Web. 29 May 2013.

12. Tom Moon. "Bruno Mars Goes Anyplace and Everyplace on 'Jukebox.'" *NPR Music*. NPR, 11 Dec. 2012. Web. 29 May 2013.

13. Melissa Maerz. "Unorthodox Jukebox." *EW.com*. Entertainment Weekly, 20 Feb. 2013. Web. 20 Apr. 2013.

14. "'Saturday Night Live': Bruno Mars Performs 'Locked Out of Heaven.'" *Huffington Post*. Huffington Post, 21 Oct. 2012. Web. 29 May 2013.

15. Jonah Weiner. "Mr. Showbiz." *Rolling Stone* 20 Jan. 2011: 50. *Zinio Digital Magazines*. Web. 20 Apr. 2013.

16. "Saturday Night Live—Haters." *NBC*. NBCUniversal, n.d. Web. 30 May 2013.

17. Elysa Gardner. "Bruno Mars Goes Back to the Future with 'Jukebox.'" *USA Today*. Gannett, 10 Dec. 2012. Web. 30 May 2013.

18. Mitchell Peters. "The Liberation Songs of Bruno Mars." *Billboard*. Prometheus Media, 6 Oct. 2012. Web. 20 Apr. 2013.

19. "Bruno Mars – When I Was Your Man." *YouTube*. YouTube, 5 Feb. 2013. Web. 30 May 2013.

20. Elysa Gardner. "Bruno Mars Goes Back to the Future with 'Jukebox.'" *USA Today*. Gannett, 10 Dec. 2012. Web. 30 May 2013.

CHAPTER 9. ROCKETING INTO THE FUTURE

1. Mitchell Peters. "The Liberation Songs of Bruno Mars." *Billboard*. Prometheus Media, 6 Oct. 2012. Web. 20 Apr. 2013.

2. George Varga. "Bruno Mars Speaks: Up to the Stars." *San Diego Union-Tribune*. San Diego Union-Tribune, 9 June 2011. Web. 31 May 2013.

3. Chris Heath. "The Mars Expedition." *GQ*. Condé Nast, Apr. 2013. Web. 20 Apr. 2013.

4. Brian Hiatt. "The Golden Child." *Rolling Stone* 9 May 2013: 40. Print.

5. Leah Greenblatt. "Bruno Mars Is Red Hot." *EW.com*. Entertainment Weekly, 17 May 2013. Web. 24 May 2013.

6. Brian Hiatt. "The Golden Child." *Rolling Stone* 9 May 2013: 43. Print.

7. "Bruno Mars Recorded A Song for His Mom When He Was 4-Heartwarming." *Cities 97*. Clear Channel Media, 3 June 2013. Web. 3 June 2013.

8. "Bruno Mars Breaks Silence on His Mother's Death." *Hollywood Reporter*. Hollywood Reporter, 7 June 2013. Web. 27 June 2013.

9. Richard Smirke. "Pop Matters." *Billboard* 23 July 2011: 23. Print.

10. Elysa Gardner. "Bruno Mars Goes Back to the Future with 'Jukebox.'" *USA Today*. Gannett, 10 Dec. 2012. Web. 30 May 2013.

11. Ibid.

12. Richard Smirke. "Pop Matters." *Billboard* 23 July 2011: 23. Print.

INDEX

INDEX CONTINUED

ABOUT THE AUTHOR

Stephanie Watson is a freelance writer based in Atlanta, Georgia. Over her 20-plus-year career, she has written for television, radio, the Web, and print. Stephanie has authored more than two dozen books, including *Celebrity Biographies: Daniel Radcliffe, Elvis Presley: Rock & Roll's King,* and *Cee Lo Green: Rapper, Singer, & Record Producer.*